WITHDRAWN

BENEATH MY HEART

BENEATH MY HEART

POETRY BY JANICE GOULD

Firebrand Books
Ithaca, New York

Several of the poems in this collection have appeared previously, some in
a slightly different form, in the following publications: *Berkeley Poetry Review,
Calyx, The Evergreen Chronicles, Fireweed, A Gathering of Spirit* (Firebrand Books),
Ikon, Living the Spirit (St. Martin's Press), *My Story's On, Naming the Waves* (Crossing
Press), *People Before Columbus,* and *Sinister Wisdom.*

Book and cover design by Betsy Bayley
Typesetting by Bets Ltd.

Printed on acid-free paper in the United States by McNauhton & Gunn

The author would like to thank the National Endowment for the Arts for a
fellowship enabling the completion of this volume.

Library of Congress Cataloging-in-Publication Data

Gould, Janice, 1949–
    Beneath my heart : poetry / by Janice Gould.
        p.   cm.
    ISBN 0–932379–85–0 : $18.95 — ISBN 0–932379–84–2 (pbk.) : $8.95
    I. Title.
PS3557.0862B46   1990
811'.54—dc20   90–13952
                                                                    CIP

In memory of my mother

Contents

COYOTISMO

Coyotismo

My mother lay on her side to birth me.
This was millennia ago
when the earth was still fresh
with the energy of being.

I was her first.
If any came before me
they were lies and unwanted.

We were poor, I was hungry.
You can't imagine the places I've begged:
beaches, city streets, conference tables.
I will eat garbage,
but not from anyone's hand.

We were poor, I was cold.
Mama made me a coat but no trousers.
People laughed at me.
I was always angry.

They joked about my sex,
said nasty things about my genitalia.
I became vengeful.

Once I heard the moon whisper behind my back.
I scooped hot coals
and threw them in her fat face.
Sure, it burned my hands—
but she is marked with permanent surprise.

Another time the night began a rumor
that I'd hump anything that moved.
What did she know? When she opened her mouth to laugh
I pulled her tongue real hard.
She vomited a trail of stars no one can clean up.

I know more than I can say!
No poetry exists which wasn't first on my lips.
I was a live seed planted by a woman
in another woman's womb.
All things insatiable belong to me.

The Beaver Woman

We meet at dusk where shadows half submerge
in the pond of my imagining.
You are the beaver woman
and I, your strange friend.

Tall grass grows by the shore.
We listen to the slow lap of water.
A bleached uprooted tree points out
a trail into the suddenly deep,
and we dive
past brown waving weeds.

Our bellies brush the soft dirt of the pond,
our toes grow hard claws.
Our hands square into paws,
our backbones curve and elongate.

The lodge is entered from below,
a doorway brightens the water.
It is warm and damp inside,
the woven floor tamped down.
Each day we gather willow sticks,
enough to winter on
when the pond freezes over.

Absorbed and stolen away
we live in the old days.
We have wandered far from home
and come to the edge of our known world.

This is a gift: to be drawn into the dark,
frightened, where power beckons,
or madness, or whatever heals.

Black Bear

One day I am a black bear,
none too friendly.
I sniff and snort down the halls of academe
looking for the woman who told me *no*.
There is scat in the stairwell,
her desk is blazed with my scratches.
I stalk her like a lover.

At night I circle and circle her house,
breathing at her windows,
pawing her doors.
Stars dot my fur,
my eyes glow with pinpoints of fire.

Lost for Years

When a bird flies in through the window
and gets trapped in your house
it's bad luck.
So are spiders seen falling from walls,
serpents kept as pets,
and bad thoughts.
Feathers, on the other hand, are signs
of health and happiness.
They are left around for our benefit.

But beware the cricket's song at night.
If you listen too closely
the sound will find its way inside
and seize your very heart.
Then you will be like Earth Initiate
who, before the beginning,
floated aimlessly out there
on the back of a turtle.
You may be lost for years.

CHILDREN WHO NEVER DEPARTED

Autobiography

I was born of a half-breed mother
and a transvestite father
on All Fools' Day
in the year of forty-nine.

I was born on a park bench
outside a museum
one morning of warm rain.
Huge ferns protected my mother and me.

I was born clutching blue light.
The weight of secrets
lolled on my infant tongue.
A stone was planted in my heart
the day of my birth.

At an early age I wanted
to run off with the gypsies
for the tambourine
and the gold hoop in my ear.
Later I wanted to join the circus
till I realized a dread of clowns
and trapeze artists.

Often I stayed away from school.

After awhile I manifested
a tendency to howl,
cry inconsolably,
and choose the wrong women.

The appendix may be consulted
for a list of lovers, pets,
travels, etc.

Three things help me get by:
a sense of navigation
unending loneliness
and black coffee.

Waiting for a Miracle

Mama and I are both the same.
Each of us wait for a miracle.
For years Mama prayed I'd change
into a normal girl. She thought
I needed an operation.
Take something out
or put something in
to make me right.

I keep saying, Mama,
it's enough of a miracle
for a person to accept herself
the way she is.

Nevertheless, I wait.
I pray to change.
And knowing I never will
I pray not to feel anymore,
anything. Make me stop
loving women,
make me not want love.
Make me change.

But no miracle occurs.

The Room

In the room where I think and think a long time,
brooding, saying nothing, where I crouch over words
because a sullen angel watches, ready to cut
my thoughts to ribbons with a fierce blade—

The room where the mirror glares back when I look in,
whose walls glow with waterstains, a room
that remains dark from undressing, from abashed crying,
where shadows tattoo the body—

In this room I stay angry and never
open the door to any stranger,
nor to you who ask to enter.

The Education

When wind sweeps the yard,
scattering the shouts of white kids,
you stand,
face pressed to the chainlink fence,
observing a world of dreams
and never enter.
I take your hand,
hold it to my chest,
and pull that mane of hair back from your face.
I tell you not to cry
because we will be friends.

Tall white girls have never felt helpless.
They have never had secrets, nor cried.
Not like us.

You and I play in the basement of our school,
in a corridor private as a mausoleum.
The bright world dims
to our quiet park
of stone floor and squeaking stairs.
Here is a broom closet where we hide,
squeezing each other's hands
till the tap of shoes is gone.

Outside, children chase one another
in wild, boy-and-girl games.
They call in hoarse voices,
making one-fingered gestures,
while we take aim
with our aggies, steelies,
and cat-eyes,
intense with concentration.

One day we will go out
and sweep the yard with our hoarse cries.
We'll chase the boys from our world of dreams,
lock them in closets in dark mausoleums,
rub them out with one-fingered gestures.
Tall white girls, pressed to the fence,
will hold our secrets to their chests.
They'll stand alone and cry.

Helpless against our rage,
we will teach them
they will never be our friends.

Children Who Never Departed

In Alaska, in the long summer twilight,
it may be when the wind's in the aspen,
the quaking leaves awaken
two Indian children
buried above the Salcha River.

They fly straight up from the grave,
and their souls wrap around each other
like a whirlwind.
Their grief falls
on the white stars of dogwood,
on spruce and willow
that bank the calm river.

Sometime you may see them
when, picking high-bush cranberries,
you sweat to the crest of a bluff.
They stand quietly at the edge of the glade,
or lie clasping one another
amid moss and matted roots
in damp exploded earth.

Doves

Our lives go on viscerally, austere, beneath our memories. You are the girl with bruised knees, her summer dress spattered with blood, grief, shame, and a man's sperm, something torn as he pushes you down on the heap of clean laundry you carried home that evening, walking barefoot on the street. I am the child who examines the body of a mourning dove in its shoebox, feathers colored ivory and blue beneath pale brown. Kneeling in the woods where moss and tall grasses grow, we know how to pray, how to have a funeral. I don't want to go there alone, or to the shed where, in the dark, bicycles are stored, and old rope.

Science Lesson

At mid-morning one November, a school bus is curbed by the park across the street from the high school. The physics class dutifully boards the bus for a field trip to the planetarium. The instructor, thin as a pencil and wearing the brown suit and white shirt of a scientist, sits at the front of the bus. On the freeway he chats with the bus driver who has dark slicked-back hair. The only thing that matters to one girl is that it is raining again, and a Friday. This, to her, is a good sign.

Outside the Museum of Natural History, the leafless trees point club-shaped branches into a windy sky. Rain sweeps in from the ocean. An Asian woman hurries along through the squall, pushing a red umbrella.

The students enter the planetarium. The false sky darkens, then deep heaven opens, revealing a universe of swirling stars, dust, gases, points of exploding brightness, a black hole of limitless proportions which pulls at them, pulls them in, students, teacher, the lady with her small umbrella, the school bus waiting on wet asphalt, all those several cold days of rain.

History Lesson

> A terrible pestilence, an intermittent fever, was reported as
> having almost depopulated the whole valley of Sacramento
> and San Joaquin . . . the country was strewn with the remains
> of the dead wherever a village had stood, and from the head-
> waters of the Sacramento to King's River only five Indians
> were seen.
>
> H. H. Bancroft

1832

All this fall we have watched our families sicken
with astonishing rapidity. In a fever they chill to the bone,
then break into a profuse sweat. The shuddering heat and cold
alternates till they are too weak to rise from where they lay
and simply die. In our village no adults are left,
just one woman so heartbroken she can do nothing
but wail and smear her shorn head with pitch.
The children not stricken with fever neither sleep nor eat.
They are frightened and grieving, for the dead
clamor about us, even in this silence,
and poison the air with their stench.
There are too many to bury. We must wander away.
We cannot stay here.

Wandering, I thought I would feel no more.
Then I came to a place that filled me with disgust and shame
though at first only confusion and fear.
The skinned carcasses of hundreds of elk
lay swelling in the rain
at the foot of the Buttes.
Two white men lived there in a canvas tent.
Up they panted when they saw me
and pointed their guns at my chest.

If I escaped it is only with a prayer,
for it seems they kill everything that goes about on legs,
and upon doing this, cut away and take the skin
and leave the meat to rot for black-winged birds of prey.

1849

General Bidwell has hired us on to work at his gold diggings
on the Feather River. If we work well we'll be paid
two red handkerchiefs a day.
Otherwise we'll be paid but one.

1851

Several headmen among us Maidu have signed a treaty
with the white government.
We are to stay on the land between Chico and Oroville,
clear up to Nimshew, and we are not to stray.
For this the men will receive a pair of jeans,
a red flannel shirt, and a plow.
Women will get a linsey gown,
a few yards of calico, scissors and thread.

1852

At first we could not understand how the whites could settle on the land granted us by the Treaty. They came in droves. Then we learned the U.S. Senate had secretly rejected all treaties with Maidu and other Indian tribes, and we were to be removed to Nome Lackie reservation, several miles away.

1863

They told us, *Because of conflict between Indians and whites*
you will be moved for your own safety to Round Valley reservation.
It is in Mendocino county, some three days march away.

The removal has taken two weeks,
and of the 461 Indians who began this miserable trek,
only 277 have come to Round Valley.
Many died as follows: Men were shot who tried to escape.
The sick, or old, or women with children
were speared if they could not keep up,
bayonettes being used to conserve ammunition.
Babies were also killed, taken by the feet
and swung against trees or rocks to crack their skulls.

1984

There are some things I don't want to think about.
That chapter, for example, on California Indians which read:
California Indians were a naturally shiftless and lazy people.
The Mission padres had no trouble bringing them into the Mission
for these Indians were more submissive than the Plains warriors.
California Indians were easily conquered.

When mama was brought to the city
she heard a neighbor remark,
"Why did they ever adopt an Indian? Don't they know
Indians are too dumb to learn anything?"
Mama said, "I'll show her!" and went off to Julliard and Columbia.
But when she came to marry my dad,
her future mother-in-law turned to him and said,
"Why, she speaks English as well as we do!"

Mama used to say, "Why can't you kids learn anything?
What's wrong with you? Are you too dumb?
Perhaps you're just lazy and stupid.
Why don't you do as well as your friends?
Why do you give up? Why do you want to fail?
Why don't you make the effort?"
But how could we answer?

Sometimes I wake up in the night clenching my fists, crying.
This morning it was because when I had to report about
Christopher Columbus, the whole class turned away, bored,
and began to talk amongst themselves.
"Christopher Columbus," I began, "had two motives
behind his voyage. He was intrigued by the discovery
of hitherto unknown languages,
and by the discovery of skull shapes and sizes
unlike the European."
Here I held up a small discolored skull, then continued,
"Christopher Columbus meant to sail around the world
until he found a language
with a shape which matched its sounds."
I held up an alphabet in beautiful calligraphy.

I knew the class did not care
and I raged into a frenzy, beating desktops,
throwing chairs aside.
The professor got up to leave the room,
her eyes sad and frightened.
I glared at her.
"You can finish your talk," she said,
"when you pull yourself together."

I stood in a corner of the room
and cried in humiliation and grief.

We Exist

For Beth Brant

Indians must be the loneliest people on Earth—
lonely from our histories,
our losses,
even those things we cannot name
which are inside us.
Our writers try to counteract the history
that says we are a dead, a conquered People.
But our words are like a shout in a blizzard.

In snow one December,
those at Wounded Knee lay dying,
dead, their mouths frozen open.
Soldiers dug a ditch
for the bodies.
Then prairie soil crumbled over the People
and their hearts fed on roots and stones.
Their mouths filled with dust.

At sunrise the daughter lies on her bed,
legs drawn up, fist in her mouth.
I am poisoned, she thinks, beneath my heart.
This is what it means to be Indian.
My mother is not here.
They mined her for her grief,
following each vein, invading
every space, removing, they said,
the last vestige of pain.

At dawn, this time of prayer, the daughter
in a voice mined from a sickness of soul,
tries to name the words
which say we exist.

Kathy's Story

Twin sisters journey to Bolivia. They are North American, and both wear thick glasses. They have traveled from the borders of Chile and Argentina, where their books were confiscated, accused by police of subversive activity. Their blue eyes are tired.

They arrive at an old inn, in whose courtyard stands a tree with gray bark full of bullet holes. The sisters eat bread and drink cocoa before retiring to their room. In their narrow beds, they fall into a deep sleep from which one is awakened late in the night by a shaking and wobbling of the bed frame. The girl half rises. "It must be an earthquake," she thinks. But then she feels the sheets and thick wool blanket being snatched from her body. She closes her eyes and tugs back.

At the foot of her bed is a lightless presence, the shape of an angry man whose life was flushed out of him one day against the tree in the courtyard.

No Nation

There is no nation in my heart.
In the canyon which was once our home
burning water springs from the rock.
We sing for the dead who leave no ghosts.

In my heart there is no nation.
Strong wind blows on our land.
The wild go wild—coyotes attack humans,
condors spite the world with their demise,
sea mammals beach themselves on an outgoing tide.

The nation in my heart is dead.
Our blood turns to powder and swirls to lightning.
Your blood burns air, too. The land flattens out.
An ash cloud forms with your passing.

A nation which never was is gone.
The lives of our dead do not trouble those who eat.
We drink from dry wells
while your grapes grow thick on the vine.
Our children cry, We *don't have no shoes.*
Your children chant, A*merica.*

THE WOMAN I LOVE MOST

Foster Family

In October rain blew in from the ocean
and came down hard in the Willamette valley.
One night it rained till midnight,
then in the morning
fog rose from the river.
The clouds lifted. We took the horses—
you on the gelding,
me on your bay mare—
and rode out to the apple orchards.

Gold light flecked the trees, the fruit,
the water in ditches.
We each rode silent,
in separate hungers.

When we turned home
it was late afternoon.
"Let's race," you said.
We'd reached the far pasture.
You dug your boot heels deep
in the gelding's flanks
and shot away. I had to follow.
Crouched low, I heard
the bay's hard breathing,
felt her sweat fly to my eyes
like the hot tears of panic
I sometimes shed.
I could see the farm lights
gleaming like faint emeralds
in the gauzy dusk.

We came in the kitchen, mud-spattered,
breathless, to steam and your family
breaking thick biscuits into their stew.
No one spoke but your old grandma
who muttered her low nonsense
till your mother's hand slapped
flat on the table.
She tore into you like a badger,
snarled the words *love*
and *lesbians*.
It was all so familiar.

I escaped to the narrow bed
your family provided, tucked
beneath a shelf of *Reader's Digests*.
I saw that night we had things in common
besides the way your face fought humiliation.

My Crush on the Yakima Woman

It was raining along the Columbia River
that November I lived on the farm.
One morning at 6:00 a.m. the Yakima woman
drove the gravel road to my place.
She had come to pick me up.

She was sure pretty, that woman,
with her wide face, obsidian eyes,
and hair the color of blackbird wings.
She had slim long legs, and every guy
at the cannery where we worked
was sick for her.
But it was me she took home
to meet her kids.

Her husband was out hunting that weekend.
I saw him only once
when he came home, changed clothes,
and went off with a beer in his hand.

She waved good-bye,
not bothering to get up.
I strummed my guitar.
She listened and smoked.
Then she said, "Sing some more."
So I threw back my head
and sang "Your Cheatin' Heart"
in a way Patsy Cline would have understood.
And the Yakima woman thought about it,
smiled, and said, "That was real good."

So I played and drank,
sang and cried. Finally
she asked, "Do you want to go to bed?"
She did not mean with her.

I slept on the sofa,
she slept in her thin chemise.
The kids slept scattered all over the floor.
About four in the morning I got up
and looked at the sky. It angered me
to see it cold and full of stars
above the black fir forest.

When Winter Hits Lake Erie

When winter hits Lake Erie and sleets the town,
the small dead lie frozen by the side of the road.
Nothing remains but torn wings, teeth,
bits of fur, and cracked bones.

When winter hits Lake Erie, you lie curled
in the ice cave which blankets your bed.
I sleep a thousand miles away in a winter all my own,

and wake to the half-human cries of coyote.
It is an effort of will to cup my hands on the window,
to peer into the dark where tracks cross the snow.

Caves

In late afternoon at the edge of a mountain
we observe light

falling across white slopes of grass
and walls of black lava.

Today I am not in love.
My words take the shape of crows

and fly off into different directions.

But she is convinced I am here
when her hand rests on my neck,

and her cool fingers
unsteady with desire,

coil in my hair.

Pointing behind us she says,
There are caves up there

where Indians would go at night
seeking visions, listening for songs.

There are burn marks
where torches flared against the rock ceiling.

Do you want to see?

I stare at damp earth,
the darkened leaves

and answer *no*.

The Woman I Love Most

The woman I love most
opens beneath her skin.
I feel the blood of her womb
waiting for me.
When she flowers,
red petals will cover parched land.
If she births monsters
we will scorch their hair,
break their strange limbs,
and shut their terrible eyes.

I want to undress
the woman I love most,
to move down her skin
at a snail's pace
leaving a trail of silver,
brave as a moon. I want to lay
my fingers on her breasts,
clasp her to me till
her breath is one with mine.

And if the woman I love most
does not love me, if
a kiss falls from her mouth
like a moth from a tree,
I will trap wild birds,
feed them lime and clay.
I will set their wings on fire
and watch them burn
till the last soft call flares away.

Tanana Valley

I spend the summer singing for you
the long walk into town
these hot mornings in Alaska.
The Tanana valley stretches
a hundred miles south
and there tremendous mountains
gleam white with snow.
Along the road fireweed burns,
bumblebees buzz in clover,
someone cuts and bales
a twelve-acre field of hay.

Sometimes in the afternoon
clouds push in over the hills,
the sky darkens, and my body
steams with sweat.
Mosquitos swarm from the dust in the road
and settle in my hair.

I watch the wild rose blossom
and the rose hip bud.
High-bush cranberries ripen
and soon the smoky hue of blueberries
will cover the muskeg bogs.

Every day my thoughts cross Canada
looking for you. Every day I wait
for your letter that never comes.

To Speak Your Name

To speak your name
between your warm thighs
above the curve of your belly
in the cave of your mouth
close to your closing eyes,
this is what I want.
My kisses scatter
like migrating birds
over your breasts.

To hold you deeper
than you have been held,
find the cry in your throat,
loosen what is lodged
in the marrow of bone and flesh,
to touch you everywhere I am
open is what I love. You
sing for me now
in your soft southern voice.

Matin

It will be cold by the window
                    in winter
before the first sun rises
above the windy river, in the crack
of dawn, through an icy glow.

Trees will stand rapt in wonder,
black against the lightening sky,
as they appear
                    this twenty-fourth of September,
the ground cold (but not so cold
as mid-December   when
the seasons turn again
ushered in by dancers, flurries
of snow, piñón fire,
and all the points of night
known and unknown).

Somewhere, here, I want
to mention the delicacy of your lips,
mouth of Catholic prayer,
tongue which takes the wafer,
finger which inscribed
a cross on my heart.

We walked in woods
under oak and alder
(the northgrowing moss,
red berries, thorns)
you in a long coat,
scarf at your throat,
your eyes watering in the cold

(for there was fog in the hollow
where the road cut deepest).
Everything was heavy with water,
unfrozen, running in courses.

Now the day's wonder begins
at the window, and a cold feeling
is etched with one warm finger
across my heart.

Blackbirds

At dusk we start home
through the wet fields.

Overhead, blackbirds flock
and flock, coming together

like the sides of a squeeze-box,
scattering apart, a rush

of stars navigating
their own universe.

The birds whisper in the damp air,
their wings breathe.

When you take my hand
I feel the pulse of their flight

in my throat, my chest.
I feel their pull

flutter through you.

Dream in November

We are on a night express
traveling through Europe.
Slumped together in the stifling air
your head rests on my shoulder.
I can see your reflection in the window:
a strand of fine hair sticks to your neck,
there's a slight flush to your face.
At dawn we will be in southern France,
or Spain, or crawling to Milan in a downpour.

The train bumps and hisses. It jars you awake.
"My eyes hurt," you say, "as if
cinders flew in them all night."
But to me they look as clear and gray as ever.
Only your cheekbones look different—sharper—
beneath your warm skin.

When we disembark my valise slips from my hand.
And you, so tired you don't want to stand,
find a bench where you can sit and wait
while I buy two coffees and a small loaf of bread.

When the rain clears we will walk through the streets.
Like immigrants we will search for a sign
that could remind us of home
and make us feel we own ourselves again.

You sip your coffee and watch passers-by.
I watch you and think of a bird in swift flight,
pushed by the wind far north of here,
how it flew toward the pale southern sky
and left no trace.

I Am Loved for My Beauty

I am Frida Kahlo with the mustached lip
and brows that knit together
black as a bat's wing.
I am Frida with the bad back of vines:
huge green leaves cover my breasts,
a briar circles my neck and pricks me
if I move my head. Drops of blood
spatter onto the wide lap of my dress.

I am Frida with the scar beneath my skirt.
Here I sit, legs apart.
If you were to lift my petticoat
you would see the sliver of wood piercing my vagina,
my stumped right foot turning inward.

I am Frida Kahlo with my hair shorn very short,
now dressed in a man's suit much too large for me.
The words of a love song ring the air behind my head
saying, I *am loved for my beauty.*
My mustached lip does not smile. It bristles.

We Look for the Deepest Green

In the jungle
we look for the deepest green.
When our bodies steam,
humid, beaded with dark water,
we dream of fish,
translucent fins and tails,
infinitesimally small roe.

The fish hide
among gold waving weeds,
pulsing softly.
In pools they wait,
stunned by the river sound,
fearful to advance.

We move upstream.
The jungle grows denser,
thick air beats against our skin.
My reptilian brain
sees life uncoil in your womb,
life with amphibian force,
turning sun and moon.

The pirogue tips slowly
upon the churning water
thick with salamanders.
Parrots scream above us,
blue-feathered and proud.
They open their ivory beaks
and beat their wings
against crumbling cliffs.

My shirt is unbuttoned,
your skin is wet.
Far off we hear air collide,
the first soft peals
rolling clouds together.
Then the sky cracks loud and white,
fierce as the breaking of trees.
Suddenly the heavens rain
frogs, bits of claw,
fish eggs,
muddy salt drops of water.
"Don't cry," I say,
but I do not know
which of us I mean.

If we travel further upstream
to Inca ruins far above the furthest cascade,
from the high stone walls
we can look down upon this verdant jungle.
We will emerge
into pale, violet light.

A Married Woman

One day you agreed to meet me
in my cold house on the hill.
You came early.
It was Saturday, raining.
I'd waited for you for days, weeks.
The evening before your visit
I'd set the table with a white cloth
and placed two purple iris
in a glass vase.
You came with your photographs and stories—
and then we made love
in my wide bed.

Outside, redwood trees scratched at the window
and rain came down
from thick rolling clouds.
We drank wine and ate bread,
we kissed and lay sleeping,
our mouths nearly touching.
Hours later, our lovemaking over,
I was restless, hungry.
I kissed the back of your neck,
stroked your thighs.
The rain was still falling.

Let's go, I said, *where there are horses.*
I was trembling with desire,
not sure how to bridge the distance.
Off we drove, slightly drunk,
with our bag of apples.

The horses were in an open field,
out in the green hills:
bay, chestnut, pinto, gray.
Come feed them, I said,
I'll show you how.

But you laughed
and wouldn't stand with me by the fence
where the horses stamped
and tossed their heads,
smelling the apples,
baring their teeth at one another
ready to nip and bite.
You were dismayed by their size,
their slobbering muzzles
and jealous natures,
the hot curious energy which brought them
to the fence and my outstretched hand.

Later you confided your fear of animals
as you lay in my arms
in the front seat of my car.
It was late and we were down
by the brown churning river.
The clouds had descended.
I thought about a fear of animals,
and then my mind went quiet.
I watched the rain batter the windshield.

AZTLÁN

January Letter

You are in a Berkeley cafe, writing
The fog today is breathy, moist.
Trees stand in it too sleepy to move.

I am miles away on a New Mexican mesa,
watching the sun move across the sky.
The air is luminous and blue.
I can feel you thinking about me.

The river swirls by, silty green.
Ice cracks along the shore, groans,
gives up its hold.
Cones burst on piñón pines,
rabbits jump in the brush.
Mountains rise above the carved, exposed earth.

In New Mexico red peppers dry
suspended from porches.
Looms are made of heavy oak,
and the weavings smell of wood and clay.

Today I miss my mother
who has been gone four months.

All of this sinks deeper than my heart.

Looking for Chamita

In 1941, Ansel Adams stepped out of his car
hurriedly set up his camera
and took a photo of Hernandez,
a village on the road to Abiquiu.
Nothing much has changed since then—
neither the moon's slow movement
nor the fluid clouds shaped like a woman's body
lying full-length over the Sangre de Cristo mountains.
The only difference is how you and I
occupy the space along the roadside.
It is a lucid night.
The ground is full of stars,
hard beneath our boots.
The smell of piñon charges the air,
and we are happy as we have never been,
hands snow cold, a clarity to our souls,
everything in black and white.
Our dream history has become possible
in this least of all possible worlds.

Our Bodies in the Half-Light

When the evening breeze rustles the curtain
and earth lets go its heat,
we lie, wet, upon your bed,
sweat-cooled, breathless,
my mouth on your breast.

Think of the acequia near our home,
cottonwoods on the bank,
shimmer of green water
beneath the vibrant grass.
How thirsty it makes us!

When the ditch floods the field,
let's bend our heads to the foam and drink.
Upturned, the earth darkens quickly,
like our bodies in the half-light.

When We Return to Aztlán

When we return to Aztlán
you will be happy.
When you remember
memories, words will form
in your mouth: lengua,
pájaro, montaño,
cloud. On your lips
at night you will speak
Aztlán, in the morning
whisper Aztlán. I will
taste it on your breasts,
smell it in your hair. All day
we will cook with chiles,
cebollas, tomates, Aztlán.
And at dusk the yard will give off
its savor of home.

BENEATH MY HEART

Three Stories from My Mother

Prayer Path

We stand beneath the buckeye tree
and the big pods rattle in the wind.
Blind grandma listens and sometimes sings
in a voice already like a ghost's.
Her hand rests on my shoulder:
I am her eyes.
I shift my weight and strain to hear
the voices she attends.

Grandma has staked the other world to our own.
The day she leaves, no longer blind,
she will follow a trail of feathers,
tassels hung to elderberry,
knots of long bent grass.
She will walk quickly
like a young thing
down the dim trail.

Cure **Night**

Mama became very sick
when something puffed in her side
like a boil.
Her limbs were soft-boned,
her eyes pockets of pain.
Finally she had no voice
to call us in from play,
so she lay down
and began to wait for death.
Papa rode out of the canyon
and brought the medicine man from Humbug Valley.

The old man chanted that night,
shaking the deerskin rattle.
He blew smoke across mama
and sucked at her sore side,
trying to draw between his teeth
what remained swollen in her.

Late in the night he stopped singing,
and in the silence
we heard the crackle of fire,
the hiss as lamps burned low.

Wind dragged itself down the creek
and seeped into the rafters of our house.
Words came in a strange high language.

The old man sighed and turned to my father,
saying no Indian medicine could change
the day of her last breath.

She Comes Home

Dad took mama up to Quincy.
White doctors removed the tumor.
Maybe because she was a half-breed
they were careless how they sewed her up.
They sent her home on the train.

Her life slipped away
as the Southern Pacific snaked down the canyon.
Its brakes groaned on the long grades,
and a hemorrhage appeared on the folds
of mama's cotton dress.
There was heat glare
on mica and serpentine.

Perhaps she watched the river,
the way it bucks and eddies
and swirls in the deep pools.
Perhaps she took in the deep blue of the sky,
noticed wind catching in the aspen,
saw patches of snow saddling the razor-back ridges.
It was thirty miles of pain
to where we kids were waiting.

At Belden station
the men strapped her to a chair
and carried her into town.
Already she was moaning
in a voice so changed and low
it belonged to no woman.

In that sound she drifted,
unaware it was death who sang.

Recovery Room

When a man is old and thinks he can rest
something swells on his head.
"I must've bumped myself," he tells his wife.
"This is a spider bite, or perhaps a bee bit me."
He waits. His head is sore
but there is no discoloration.
One night he says to his wife,
"Have you changed my pillow?"
She replies, "No."
He gets up
and wanders around his house.
He takes aspirin and sits in his chair.
Near dawn he falls asleep
with the cat in his lap.

When a man is old and his heart isn't good
he must go in for an operation.
In the hospital the man says,
"Doctor, don't put me on that life support.
If I'm going to die, let me."

Now the doctors are ready
and the man is wheeled away.
The hours pass, the family waits.
Then the surgeon returns and announces,
"We didn't get it all.
Still, it cannot reach his brain."

In the recovery room the man moans.
He rises in his sleep
and tries to struggle from his bed.

A gray wolf snaps at his bare heels.

Mama at the Hospital

Mama lies on her side in the hospital bed
in a room somber as our church.
She breathes a strange sleep,
as if all her life her hands were cupped
before her as they are now,
neither numb nor alive,
but in a quiet place
further than dreams.

The hospital gown is unhappy on her small frame,
and surely her brown feet lie tucked and hot
under the hard sheets.

We touch her temples,
pat the loose strands of hair
away from her smooth face.

She does not wake
nor wrap her fingers around our own.

Questions of Healing

In Dorothy Hill's *The Fauna and Flora of the Mountain Maidu*,
I turn a page and discover
the healing properties of cedar,
elderberry and spruce,
of deer hooves, eagle's bones, and sage.

In times past
all things helped the People survive.
For each thing that harmed—
rattler, poison oak, grizzly bear, lightning—
another thing existed to cure, arrest poison,
reverse madness, disease, or death.

To imagine that the world could exist
so finely balanced!
Each day to strike fire from a stone,
and watch clouds gather at the canyon's edge.
To see smoke rise from the volcano
and believe in the rightness
and clear gifts of the earth.
To calmly face our own aging—
how strange and inaccessible.

When I watched my mother die
with no recourse to laurel,
sweet birch or pine, no baskets
to burn on the pyre in October (ourselves
the sticks of charcoal, shaved heads,
black face, purified by smoke),
I found only half-questions:
What in our world? How close to death?
What can change? What have I lost?

Last Journey

Mama left for the mountains
on the first of September.
She traveled west to east,
an old journey through manzanita,
sage and rabbit brush.

In canyons, oak leaves shimmered
in dry heat,
cones dropped from sugar pines
in a scatter of small brown wings.
Mama followed a streambed
of flat white stones.

When you passed the Buttes, mama,
did you pray for your daughters
whose way to the meadows above
might be difficult?

Up there, beyond black mesas
and eroded cliffs
is the red earth country
of our home.

Beneath My Heart

I felt the soul move within my body
and placed my hands over my heart,

but my soul drifted
effortlessly out of my grasp.

It hovered above me like a shadow
caught in a leafless tree.

Below my breast I searched,
trying to find the heart's beat.

Grace drags the soul,
deadened like a numb foot

out of its earthlike sleep,

while light, heavy as flame,
breaks through the trees.

Beneath my heart a torrent of blood
carries all that I love.

When mama dies I will turn
like a star learning to shine,

the world will release me
into its vastness.

When death comes rapping with its soft claw,
I will stand in the doorway,
then leave.

Other titles from Firebrand Books include:

The Big Mama Stories by Shay Youngblood/$8.95

A Burst Of Light, Essays by Audre Lorde/$7.95

Crime Against Nature, Poetry by Minnie Bruce Pratt/$8.95

Diamonds Are A Dyke's Best Friend by Yvonne Zipter/$9.95

Dykes To Watch Out For, Cartoons by Alison Bechdel/$6.95

Exile In The Promised Land, A Memoir by Marcia Freedman/$8.95

Eye Of A Hurricane, Stories by Ruthann Robson / $8.95

The Fires Of Bride, A Novel by Ellen Galford/$8.95

A Gathering Of Spirit, A Collection by North American Indian Women edited by Beth Brant (*Degonwadonti*)/$9.95

Getting Home Alive by Aurora Levins Morales and Rosario Morales/$8.95

Good Enough To Eat, A Novel by Lesléa Newman/$8.95

Humid Pitch, Narrative Poetry by Cheryl Clarke/$8.95

Jewish Women's Call For Peace edited by Rita Falbel, Irena Klepfisz, and Donna Nevel/$4.95

Jonestown & Other Madness, Poetry by Pat Parker/$7.95

The Land Of Look Behind, Prose and Poetry by Michelle Cliff/$6.95

A Letter To Harvey Milk, Short Stories by Lesléa Newman/$8.95

Letting In The Night, A Novel by Joan Lindau/$8.95

Living As A Lesbian, Poetry by Cheryl Clarke/$7.95

Making It, A Woman's Guide to Sex in the Age of AIDS by Cindy Patton and Janis Kelly/$4.95

Metamorphosis, Reflections On Recovery, by Judith McDaniel/$7.95

Mohawk Trail by Beth Brant (*Degonwadonti*)/$7.95

Moll Cutpurse, A Novel by Ellen Galford/$7.95

More Dykes To Watch Out For, Cartoons by Alison Bechdel/$7.95

The Monarchs Are Flying, A Novel by Marion Foster/$8.95

Movement In Black, Poetry by Pat Parker/$8.95

My Mama's Dead Squirrel, Lesbian Essays on Southern Culture by Mab Segrest/$8.95

(continued)

New, Improved! Dykes To Watch Out For, Cartoons by Alison Bechdel/$7.95

The Other Sappho, A Novel by Ellen Frye/$8.95

Politics Of The Heart, A Lesbian Parenting Anthology edited by Sandra Pollack and Jeanne Vaughn/$11.95

Presenting . . . Sister NoBlues by Hattie Gossett/$8.95

A Restricted Country by Joan Nestle/$8.95

Sacred Space by Geraldine Hatch Haron/$9.95

Sanctuary, A Journey by Judith McDaniel/$7.95

Sans Souci, And Other Stories by Dionne Brand/$8.95

Scuttlebutt, A Novel by Jana Williams/$8.95

Shoulders, A Novel by Georgia Cotrell/$8.95

Simple Songs, Stories by Vickie Sears/$8.95

The Sun Is Not Merciful, Short Stories by Anna Lee Walters/$7.95

Tender Warriors, A Novel by Rachel Guido deVries/$8.95

This Is About Incest by Margaret Randall/$7.95

The Threshing Floor, Short Stories by Barbara Burford/$7.95

Trash, Stories by Dorothy Allison/$8.95

The Women Who Hate Me, Poetry by Dorothy Allison/$5.95

Words To The Wise, A Writer's Guide to Feminist and Lesbian Periodicals & Publishers by Andrea Fleck Clardy/$4.95

Yours In Struggle, Three Feminist Perspectives on Anti-Semitism and Racism by Elly Bulkin, Minnie Bruce Pratt, and Barbara Smith/$8.95

You can buy Firebrand titles at your bookstore, or order them directly from the publisher (141 The Commons, Ithaca, New York 14850, 607-272-0000).

Please include $1.75 shipping for the first book and $.50 for each additional book.

A free catalog is available on request.